DANGEROUS DUNG

by
Charis Mather

Minneapolis, Minnesota

Credits

Images are courtesy of Shutterstock.com. With thanks to GettyImages, ThinkstockPhoto, and iStockphoto.

Cover – Vector_Up, irin-k, Eric Isslee. Recurring images – gravity_point, yugoro, The_Pixel, lyeyee, Voin_Sveta, nataliiudina, ozzichka, johnjohnson. 2–3 – Sorbis. 4–5 – Eric Isselee, VP Photo Studio. 6–7 – Ethan Daniels, Laura Dts. 8–9 – Francisco Blanco, Svetlana Foote. 10–11 – aaltair, frank60, photowind. 12–13 – Emőke Dénes (Wikimedia Commons), Jose Barquero. J. 14–15 – Jesus Cobaleda, Nick Pecker. 16–17 – Agnieszka Bacal, Debbie Steinhausser, Anna Violet. 18–19 – Agami Photo Agency, John Navajo, Vishnevskiy Vasily. 20–21 – Chanasid kaewpirun, Novim images. 22–23 – Keri Delaney, Rob Hainer.

Library of Congress Cataloging-in-Publication Data

Names: Mather, Charis, 1999- author.
Title: Dangerous dung / by Charis Mather.
Description: Minneapolis, Minnesota : Bearport Publishing Company, [2024] | Series: Beastly wildlife | Includes index.
Identifiers: LCCN 2023031025 (print) | LCCN 2023031026 (ebook) | ISBN 9798889163398 (library binding) | ISBN 9798889163442 (paperback) | ISBN 9798889163480 (ebook)
Subjects: LCSH: Animal droppings--Juvenile literature.
Classification: LCC QL768 .M379 2024 (print) | LCC QL768 (ebook) | DDC 591.47/9--dc23/eng/20230713
LC record available at https://lccn.loc.gov/2023031025
LC ebook record available at https://lccn.loc.gov/2023031026

© 2024 BookLife Publishing
This edition is published by arrangement with BookLife Publishing.

North American adaptations © 2024 Bearport Publishing Company. All rights reserved. No part of this publication may be reproduced in whole or in part, stored in any retrieval system, or transmitted in any form or by any means, electronic, mechanical, photocopying, recording, or otherwise, without written permission from the publisher.

For more information, write to Bearport Publishing, 5357 Penn Avenue South, Minneapolis, MN 55419.

CONTENTS

Beastly! 4
Dirty Droppings 6
Staying Safe 8
Dog Walking Dangers 10
Watch Your Feet! 12
Disgusting Dinners 14
Bathroom Builders 16
Hip-poo-potamuses 18
Strangely Shaped Scat 20
Dreadfully Dangerous Dung 22
Glossary 24
Index 24

BEASTLY!

If you've ever had a pet, you might think you know a lot about dung. However, there is more to this stinky subject than most people realize.

THERE'S MORE TO KNOW ABOUT MY POO?

There are all sorts of animals in the world, and many have some beastly bathroom behavior. So, plug your nose and read on . . . if you dare!

DIRTY DROPPINGS

The different names for dung might make you giggle. Have you heard it called muck, poo, scat, or doo-doo? Silly names or not, these dirty droppings aren't just a joke. They can can spread nasty **diseases**.

Soap gets rid of lots of bacteria. That is why you should also wash your hands before you eat. Otherwise, you might end up taking a bite out of a bacteria burger. *Yuck!*

DOG WALKING DANGERS

Dog poop is pretty gross on its own. But to make it worse, sometimes it's full of tiny eggs. These aren't the kind of eggs you scramble for breakfast. These are roundworm eggs!

Roundworms are **parasites** that live inside other animals . . . even humans! Just a little bit of wormy poo near another creature's mouth is dangerous. Once swallowed, the eggs **hatch**, and roundworms grow inside the unlucky animal.

Sometimes, roundworms can live in a creature's stomach for years without being noticed.

NEW HOME WANTED

WATCH YOUR FEET!

Poo is pretty horrible stuff. However, some animals do not seem bothered by it. In fact, turkey vultures poop on their feet on purpose! *Pee-yew!*

A turkey vulture's feet look white because they are covered in poop.

Pooping on their own feet helps turkey vultures cool down in hot weather. Strangely, a strong **acid** in their poop also kills the bacteria that gets on their feet from the rotting animals they eat.

DISGUSTING DINNERS

Some animals snack on scat. *Munch!* Who would want to eat that?

The first food baby koalas eat is their mothers' poo. This helps their **guts** get ready to eat eucalyptus leaves when they are older.

I CANNOT WAIT TO GROW UP....

Rabbits have two different kinds of poop. One kind is dry, and the other is wet and sticky. Surprisingly, eating the stickier waste is very good for them.

Dry poop

Sticky poop

Dung beetles do more than just eat waste. Some also live in dung. They lay their eggs there, too.

Bathroom BUILDERS

Not all animals have disgusting bathroom **habits**. In fact, some badger groups dig shared toilet areas called latrines.

WHO USED THE LAST BIT OF TOILET PAPER?

HIP-POO-POTAMUSES

Hippopotamuses eat about 90 pounds (40 kg) of plants every day. Lots of food means lots of poop. And these large animals are not shy about letting their waste fly.

STRANGELY SHAPED SCAT

Hippos are not the only animals that mark their territory with poop. Wombats do, too. However, wombat scat is much smaller and drier . . . and it is cube shaped!

HMM, WHERE SHOULD I LEAVE THE NEXT ONE?

Wombats often leave their smelly markers on top of rocks. Since their poop has flat sides, it does not roll away easily. Wombats can make up to 100 poopy cubes a day.

DREADFULLY DANGEROUS DUNG

There is much more to animal muck than meets the eye . . . or the nose. These beastly bathroom habits might be gross, but they are also awfully interesting.

> I REALLY DO NOT KNOW WHAT ALL THE FUSS IS ABOUT.

From dangerous dung full of roundworm eggs to cute little cubes, this smelly subject is a pile of fun. Although you might not think that next time you accidentally step in something brown!

GLOSSARY

acid a substance that can be dangerous and cause harm

bacteria living things too small to see that can cause sickness

diseases illnesses

guts organs inside the bodies of animals

habits activities that people or animals do often

hatch to come out of eggs

parasites living things that live on or in other living things and harm them

territory an area of land where an animal lives

INDEX

bacteria 7, 9, 13
cubes 20-21, 23
diseases 6
eat 9, 13-15, 17-18
eggs 10-11, 15, 23
feet 12-13
latrines 16
nest 17
soap 8-9
territory 19-20